W9-BOL-857

Editor: PENNY CLARKE
Artists: MARK BERGIN
        DAVID ANTRAM

Produced by
THE SALARIYA BOOK CO. LTD
25 Marlborough Place
Brighton BN1 5UB
England

Published by
PETER BEDRICK BOOKS
2112 Broadway
New York, NY 10023

Published by agreement with
Macdonald Young Books Ltd, England

Library of Congress Cataloging-in-Publication
Data

Macdonald, Fiona.
    First facts about the American frontier / written by Fiona
Macdonald : illustrated by Mark Bergin : created and designed
by David Salariya.
        p.   cm.
    Includes index.
    Summary: Presents facts about life for the nineteenth-
century pioneers on the American frontier.
    ISBN 0-87226-498-X
    1. Frontier and pioneer life--West (U.S.)--Juvenile literature.
2. West (U.S.)--History--Juvenile literature.   [1. Frontier
and pioneer life--West (U.S.) 2. West (U.S.)--History.]
I. Bergin, Mark, ill.   II. Salariya, David.   III. Title.
F596.M138   1996
978--dc20   96-12297
                                      CIP
                                      AC

Printed in Hong Kong.

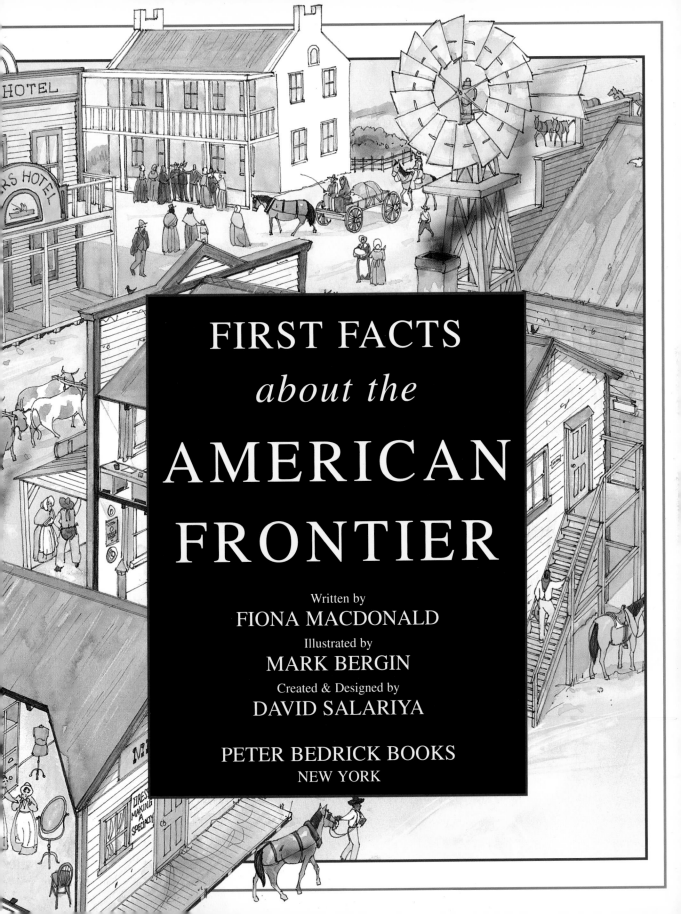

FIRST FACTS
about the
AMERICAN
FRONTIER

Written by
FIONA MACDONALD

Illustrated by
MARK BERGIN

Created & Designed by
DAVID SALARIYA

PETER BEDRICK BOOKS
NEW YORK

Contents

INTRODUCTION

THE STORY of the American frontier is both a triumph and a tragedy. The triumph belongs to thousands of 19th century pioneers. They left their homes in the eastern states of America or distant northern Europe and made the long trek overland to build new towns, ranches and farms on lands to the west of the Mississippi River. The risks were enormous, but they were spurred on by a spirit of adventure, by the need to escape from poverty, or by the wish to 'get rich quick'. Some were inspired by a strong Christian faith. Many believed in 'Manifest Destiny' – the idea that God was arranging a great future for the new nation of the USA, and that they had a part to play in building this future by bringing American 'civilization' to 'wild' western lands.

The tragedy belongs to the Native American people, who lost their homes, their lands and their lives in an unequal struggle against pioneer ranchers and farmers, backed by the US Army. To the pioneers, Native American lifestyles seemed primitive and savage. But in fact the Native American civilization was very rich. It had evolved over thousands of years to enable Native peoples to survive in a variety of harsh environments, living (on the whole) in harmony with nature in their splendid land. Native American civilization was almost destroyed – but not quite. It survived and today it is admired and celebrated.

FACT: THERE WERE SOME 300 NATIVE AMERICAN NATIONS

tomahawk

ALASKA

spear

drum

DRUM, spear and tomahawk of a Great Plains warrior.

totem pole

elk

wolf

bald eagle

Rocky Mountains

grizzly bear

Th

NORTH AMERICA is a vast land. It has frozen tundra in the Arctic north and hot dry deserts in the far south-west. Once, deer, wolves and grizzly bears lived in the forests, and huge herds of buffalo roamed the grasslands known as the Great Plains.

By 1500, around 300 Native nations lived in North America, including the Sioux and Comanche from the Great Plains, the Paiute and Apache from the south-west, the Hopi from New Mexico, the Cherokee from Georgia and the Huron and Algonquians from the north-east.

Facts about Early America:

The earliest inhabitants arrived in America about 30,000 years ago. They crossed a land-bridge linking Siberia and Alaska. Many fine civilizations flourished in North and South America. Around 1400, the Incas ruled Peru. The Maya and the Aztecs lived in Mexico from 300-1500. Rich city-states grew up in the Mississippi Valley from 800-1200. The Anasazi of the south-west built magnificent communal villages around 1000-1300.

PACIFIC OCEAN

IN the south-west, the Hopi lived in mud-brick villages called 'pueblos'.

MEXICO

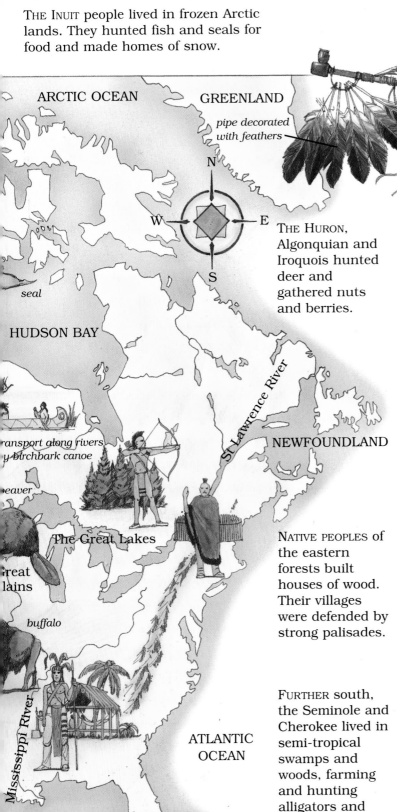

THE INUIT people lived in frozen Arctic lands. They hunted fish and seals for food and made homes of snow.

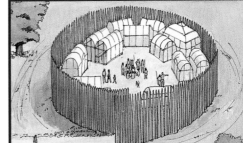

A TOBACCO PIPE and hunting knife made by people living on the Great Plains.

pipe decorated with feathers

hunting knife

ARCTIC OCEAN

GREENLAND

N

W — E

S

seal

HUDSON BAY

THE HURON, Algonquian and Iroquois hunted deer and gathered nuts and berries.

transport along rivers by birchbark canoe

beaver

St Lawrence River

NEWFOUNDLAND

The Great Lakes

Great Plains

buffalo

NATIVE PEOPLES of the eastern forests built houses of wood. Their villages were defended by strong palisades.

Mississippi River

ATLANTIC OCEAN

FURTHER south, the Seminole and Cherokee lived in semi-tropical swamps and woods, farming and hunting alligators and crabs.

GULF OF MEXICO

POMEIOC, an Algonquian village in present-day North Carolina, sketched by John White, an English traveler, in 1585.

THE far western desert is one of the hottest places on earth.

THE majestic Rocky Mountains stretch from north to south.

THE Mississippi River runs 2,348 miles south to the sea.

THE Great Plains are wide, rolling grasslands where few trees grow.

FACT: NO PART OF A BUFFALO WAS WASTED

NATIVE AMERICAN PEOPLES living in different regions developed very different lifestyles. In the north, they lived by fishing; in the east, they hunted and farmed; in the far south-west, they gathered wild food from the desert; on the Great Plains, some settled in villages, and grew maize, beans and squash. Others lived as nomads in summer, roaming the prairies hunting the buffalo that grazed on the tall grass. In winter, they lived in teepee camps. These lifestyles changed after European settlers arrived.

NATIVE AMERICANS bred their horses to be fast, obedient and brave. They were trained to gallop close behind a buffalo on its left-hand side, so the leading rider in a team of hunters would have both hands free to shoot arrows right into the buffalo's heart. Buffalo were very strong. Only an arrow through the heart would result in a certain kill.

Settlers took over eastern Native lands, forcing the people west. 16th-century Spanish settlers had brought horses (the original American horse was extinct), which enabled Great Plains nomads to roam further than before.

Facts about Using a Buffalo:

Every part of a dead buffalo was used: muscles and brains were eaten. Hides made rugs, teepees, shoes and clothes. Hair was used for decoration, woven into cloth or twisted into ropes. Horns and bones made weapons, tools and jewelry. Tongues were eaten or used as hairbrushes. Tails made fly whisks; hooves were boiled for glue; the stomach and bladder made bags.

NATIVE AMERICANS believed that all life was sacred, and that animals should only be killed for food or as a religious sacrifice. After a successful chase hunters gave thanks to the Great Spirit, and honored the dead buffalo, too.

NATIVE AMERICAN horses were painted with magic signs, to protect them when hunting or in battle. Each warrior used his own special signs.

FACT: GUNS, KNIVES AND WHISKEY RUINED MANY LIVES

THE FIRST EUROPEANS in America settled along the east coast. But, by 1700, they were beginning to spread westward. At the same time, European hunters ranged the woods, killing animals for their skins and furs. They were so 'successful' that, after 1840, there were few beavers left. European traders began visiting frontier forts and started trading with Native American nations. Other travelers had scientific aims. Geographers like Alexander Mackenzie, who crossed Canada in 1792-1793, hoped to survey the landscape and make accurate maps. European artists recorded Native people, wildlife and scenery. After the USA acquired vast western territories from France in 1803, the government employed the explorers Lewis and Clark to make the first journey across America in 1804-1806.

AFTER the dead buffalo had been skinned the women prepared the hides by scraping them clean, then greasing and drying them.

CARVED wooden bowls used by the Sioux nation for feasts. The one in front is made of ash, the other is maple.

EUROPEAN traders sold cheap goods – such as glass beads and brightly colored blankets – to the Native nations at very high prices.

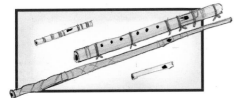

WHISTLES and flutes were carved from wood or bone. After dark, Native American boys played tunes on their whistles outside the teepees of girls they hoped to marry. If a girl sang back, it showed she liked the boy.

NOMAD nations of the Great Plains made their homes in teepees – tents of buffalo skin stretched over wooden poles.

Facts about Western Trade:

Goods traded by Europeans transformed many Native American lives. Some trade goods were harmless, but European guns, knives and whiskey all did great harm. Even 'safe' trade goods, such as blankets and beads, led to the loss of traditional Native craft skills.

Native Americans welcomed traders and guests with gifts of food. After a deal was agreed, everyone shared a pipe filled with tobacco – for Native Americans, a sacred herb.

NATIVE Americans did not have wheeled transport. For carrying heavy loads they used a travois – a frame of long poles (above).

INSIDE, teepees were warm and cozy, with a buffalo-dung fire burning in a ring of stones, and buffalo-skin rugs to sit on.

FACT: SOME NATIVE AMERICANS JOINED THE US ARMY

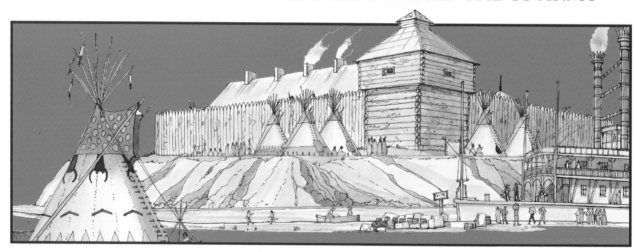

IN 1755, British colonial officials offered a reward for every scalp belonging to a dead Native American from an 'enemy nation'. This was the latest move in the wars between European settlers and Native peoples. As the settlers moved west, they made friends with some Native nations, but became enemies of others. Along the frontier between 'wild' and cultivated land, the army built forts to protect the settlers. Each fort was a little town, with lodgings, stables and a shop.

Facts about Fort Life:
Forts were extremely unhealthy places. More soldiers died from diseases caused by poor food and bad sanitation than from injuries received in war.

Native Americans sometimes worked for the army as interpreters or scouts, especially when the army was fighting against their nation's own enemies.

general

private soldier
ready for duty

cavalryman
in frontier clothes

Native American
scout

cavalryman on
stable duty

THE GENERAL commanded the regiment. Below him were captains who led 25 men.

CAVALRYMEN fought on horseback with guns and swords. They rode long distances in wild, western country.

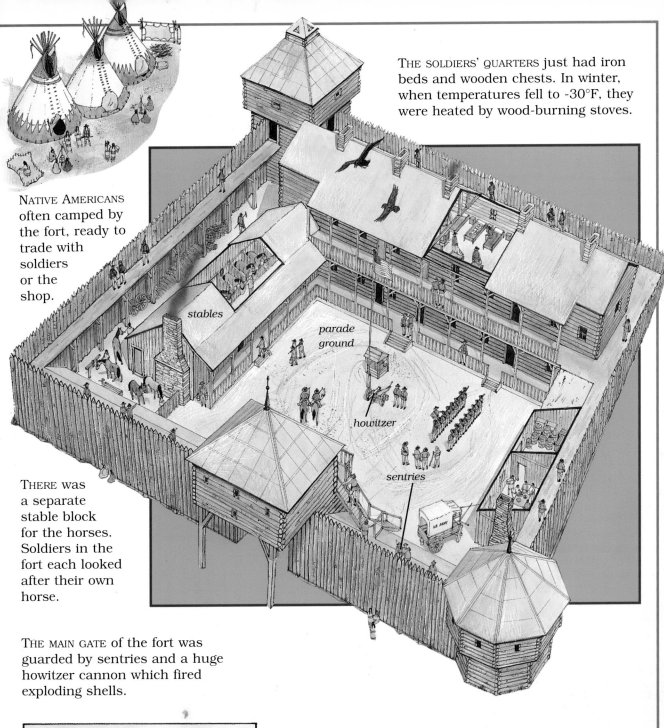

THE SOLDIERS' QUARTERS just had iron beds and wooden chests. In winter, when temperatures fell to -30°F, they were heated by wood-burning stoves.

NATIVE AMERICANS often camped by the fort, ready to trade with soldiers or the shop.

stables

parade ground

howitzer

sentries

THERE was a separate stable block for the horses. Soldiers in the fort each looked after their own horse.

THE MAIN GATE of the fort was guarded by sentries and a huge howitzer cannon which fired exploding shells.

GUARDS kept a constant lookout from the gallery which ran inside the fort's wooden walls. The treeless Great Plains landscape made it easy to spot a cloud of dust stirred up by approaching men and horses but, until the riders were close, guards could not tell whether they were enemies or friends.

SOLDIERS spent hours drilling (practicing marching and fighting techniques) on the open parade ground inside the fort (above).

FACT: SOLDIERS WORE SECOND-HAND CLOTHES

A SOLDIER'S LIFE was a mixture of boredom and danger. In wartime, out on patrol, he faced sudden death from Native American arrows at any moment. But in peacetime there was not much to do, just mending, cooking, cleaning and drill. He only got paid every two months, but in a remote fort there was little to buy – the shop sold few luxuries, just coffee and tobacco.

TROOPS ate plenty of meat. Soldiers shot buffalo and elk which roamed nearby, or bought carcases from Native American hunters. Some forts kept cows and pigs.

THE FORT had no refrigerator. In summer meat was salted to preserve it. In winter, food left out of doors froze overnight.

TURKEYS and chickens gave eggs and meat.

SOME forts hired gardeners to grow vegetables for the troops; at other forts, soldiers took turns at garden duty. Crops included melons, sqash, apples, corn and beans. But, whoever grew the food, the soldiers had to cook it themselves (above).

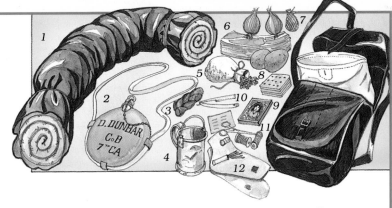

Facts about Army Life:

Soldiers were given an allowance to buy clothing. To save money, they bought second-hand uniforms, which might be thin, faded and patched.

Most soldiers could not read or write, but Fort Laramie had a school.

African-Americans joined the US Army and fought on the western frontier. They faced racial prejudice, but won praise for their courage.

SOLDIERS leaving the fort packed their field sack (far right) with essential kit: 1 Rolled blanket. 2 Water bottle ('canteen'). 3 Chewing tobacco. 4 Tin mug. 5 Coffee beans. 6 Bacon. 7 Onions. 8 Potatoes. 9 Hard biscuits. 10 Razor. 11 Matches. 12 Sewing kit.

ARMY food could be very nasty – burned, tasteless or undercooked. But at least, in the fort, there was always enough to eat. Favorite army foods included stew, baked beans, salt pork – and pancakes for breakfast. Soldiers on campaign often faced hunger and thirst.

6:30AM Time to get up and dress.

WASH, put on heavy army boots.

RECEIVE orders from sergeant.

AT work, mending vital army road.

A PICNIC LUNCH (left) of very hard biscuits, apples and cheese.

OFF-DUTY (right). Time for a game of baseball.

17

FACT: LONG WAGON TRAINS WERE HARDER TO ATTACK

CHILDREN leaving the eastern states to start a new life in the West took their favorite toys, like this rag doll, for comfort on the long trek.

BY 1800, European-Americans living in the east were eager for more land. Regular boatloads of settlers from Europe meant that land was becoming expensive and scarce. Then, reports from explorers revealed that the 'Wild West' was a magnificent territory, full of opportunity for those prepared to make the long, risky trek. So pioneer wagon trains set off in search of cheap land and new homes.

In 1787, the US government had decreed that Native peoples' 'property, rights and liberty . . . never shall be . . . disturbed.' Sadly, this law was almost completely ignored. During the 19th century Native American homelands were taken away, and handed over, with government consent, to wagon-train pioneers.

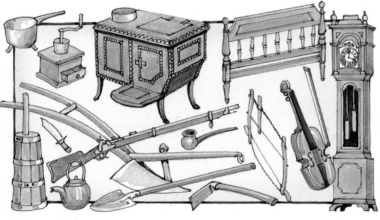

PIONEERS had to take everything they might need with them. For years, there were no shops or factories in the West. Essentials included cooking stoves, pots, farm tools, books, clothes, furniture, home-made medicines and musical instruments.

Facts about Wagon Trains:

Native warriors would wreck wagon trains by stampeding buffalo herds towards them, although long trains were harder to wreck in this way.

Wagon trains set off in May, as soon as there was enough grass on the prairies to feed the oxen and mules. The pioneers had to reach their destination before the first snow fell in October. If they had not crossed the Rocky Mountains by then, they and their animals would freeze or starve to death.

OXEN travel about 12 miles a day, so the journey from the eastern states to the West, a distance of over 2,000 miles, took about 5 months. Thirst, illness, accidents, starvation and attacks by Native Americans often slowed the wagon train, or halted it altogether. Wagons had no springs or brakes, so the journey along rutted tracks was very uncomfortable.

WAGON TRAINS passed through desolate country, often in temperatures of over 95°F, without shade or fresh water. Many pioneers and their animals died. They were buried by the side of the trail.

WAGON wheels were fixed to cone-shaped axles. These kept the wheels turning straight.

WAGONS had two big rear wheels to carry the load, and two small front ones to make the wagon easier to turn and steer.

WAGONS were covered by canvas sheets, tied over tall wooden hoops. The canvas was coated with linseed oil to make it waterproof.

WAGONS were pulled by oxen or (rarely) by mules. Oxen were cheaper and stronger. Teams of four or six oxen were harnessed in pairs to wooden yokes (below).

PADDED leather collars (below) helped mules to pull heavy wagon-loads.

FACT: FARMERS STARVED IF THE CROPS FAILED

NOT ALL LAND in the American West was suitable for farming. The best land was on the rolling prairie grasslands of the Great Plains or far beyond the Rocky Mountains. Prairie land was fertile, but the weather was extreme. In summer it could be over 90°F with fierce thunderstorms; in winter it was well below freezing with deep drifts of snow. Farmers often made disastrous mistakes, such as relying on a single crop. Wheat, for example, fetched high prices, but was quite difficult to grow. If the crop failed because of disease or bad weather, the farmer had nothing to sell. In bad years some farming families even starved to death.

THE FARM YEAR began with clearing grass and plowing the soil.

THEN winter wheat was sown. Rich farmers used mechanized drills.

AT MIDSUMMER, everyone helped cut hay for cattle food in the winter.

IN LATE summer, the farmer and his family worked hard to harvest the wheat.

PRAIRIE CROPS
Farmers grew corn, wheat, potatoes, sorghum and melons. They raised cattle, sheep and pigs. They also hunted Great Plains' wildlife for extra food, skins and furs.

PLOWING was exhausting work. Prairie grasses had roots which made a tangled mass about 10 inches deep. Farmers used special plows to cut through the roots to the rich soil.

corn

wheat

cattle

beaver

prairie chicken

antelope

wild cat

mink

potatoes

sorghum

hog

racoon

wild turkey

deer

melon

sheep and sheepdog

Facts about Farming:

Farmers laid claim to (free) new land by plowing a furrow or putting a fence all round the boundary. Then they had to register their claim at a government office in the nearest town.

African-Americans migrated from the southern states of the USA to work as farmers on the Great Plains.

The Great Plains soil was rich, but new farmers plowed up all the original vegetation, the top soil dried out, turned to dust and blew away in the wild prairie winds.

As well as severe weather, farmers faced locust swarms, rattlesnakes, poisonous plants and grass fires.

Barbed wire was invented in 1874, by a farmer, Joseph Glidden. Fences kept cattle out of crops, but ruined Native Americans' hunting grounds.

Farmers in the south-west were cattle ranchers, raising beef cattle on the dusty, semi-desert lands.

Cattle were branded with their owner's mark. Each year they were rounded up, loaded on to trains and sent east to provide cheap food for city-dwellers.

Water was essential for all western farms. It was raised by wind-pumps.

rancher

branding iron

cowboy

FACT: MANY PIONEER FAMILIES LIVED IN EARTH HOUSES

PIONEER FAMILIES were often very poor. They had spent all their money hiring a wagon and oxen, and on food for the long journey westward. When they reached the Great Plains, they found that land was cheap, but that almost everything else, including building materials, was very expensive, because it had to be transported such long distances. There were no trees and very little building stone. How could they afford a house for their families?

Many Native Americans on the Great Plains lived in teepee camps. But others, like the Mandan, lived in villages built of cozy 'earth lodges' – big, solid buildings, made of hard-packed turf and mud. And so pioneers followed their example, and built their new farmhouses out of slabs (or 'sods') of turf, as well.

LEFT: Small, simple sod houses (top) were built into the hillside. L-shaped sod houses (middle) had more space inside. Cabins built of wood (bottom) were more comfortable than sod houses, but wood was scarce.

ONLY the richest farmers could afford log cabins.

Facts about Farmhouses:
Autumn was the best time to build a sod house. The roots of the prairie grass were strongest then.

The inside walls were covered with a mixture of ashes and grey clay. This was supposed keep insects away.

It took about 2 acres of turf to build a one-roomed sod house.

Doors and windows were bought by mail order, and delivered to the nearest town.

TURF for building sod houses was cut from prairie land that had never been plowed. Farmers used sharpened shovels to cut thick slabs of grass, roots and soil.

SLABS OF TURF were laid grass side down. Some of the grass roots continued to grow; they helped to bind the slabs together and make the walls strong. Turf walls were very thick – even so, they might be washed away by heavy rain. Roofs were also made of turf, laid over wooden rafters. Grass and wild flowers grew on top. Rats, snakes and insects lived inside.

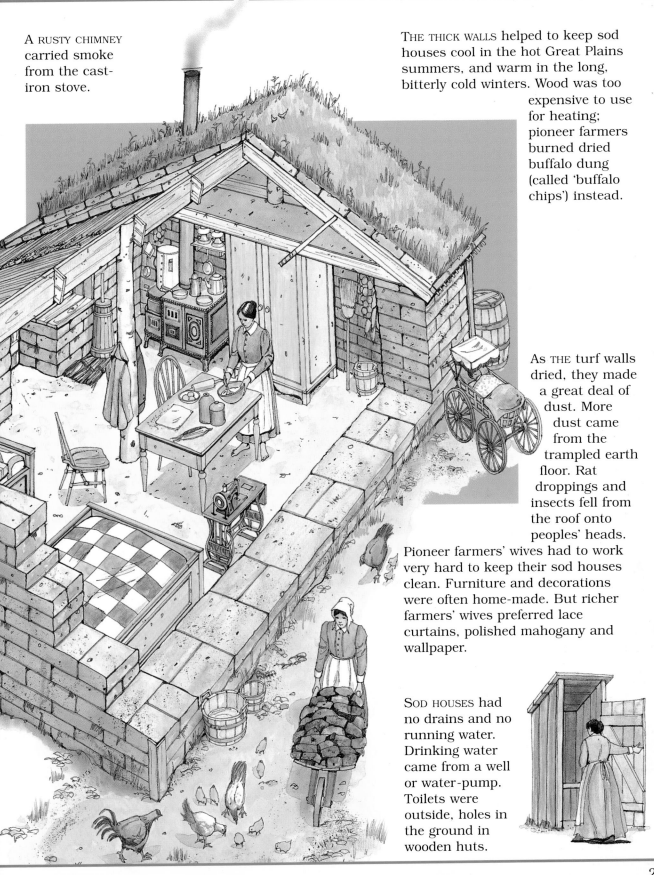

A RUSTY CHIMNEY carried smoke from the cast-iron stove.

THE THICK WALLS helped to keep sod houses cool in the hot Great Plains summers, and warm in the long, bitterly cold winters. Wood was too expensive to use for heating; pioneer farmers burned dried buffalo dung (called 'buffalo chips') instead.

As THE turf walls dried, they made a great deal of dust. More dust came from the trampled earth floor. Rat droppings and insects fell from the roof onto peoples' heads. Pioneer farmers' wives had to work very hard to keep their sod houses clean. Furniture and decorations were often home-made. But richer farmers' wives preferred lace curtains, polished mahogany and wallpaper.

SOD HOUSES had no drains and no running water. Drinking water came from a well or water-pump. Toilets were outside, holes in the ground in wooden huts.

FACT: RAILROADS WERE LIFELINES FOR FRONTIER TOWNS

PONY EXPRESS messengers rode 75 mile relays most days, whatever the weather.

BEFORE the railroad and telegraph came to the American West in the 1860s, relays of Wells Fargo Pony Express' riders carried urgent messages from town to town.

THOUSANDS of Chinese and Irish workers were recruited to clear the route for the railroad and lay the track. Iron rails were laid on timber sleepers, placed across a level bed of stones.

THE FIRST railroads in the USA were built in 1829, in the eastern states. Building stopped during the American Civil War (1861-1865). But after the war a railroad 'boom' began.

Railroads helped open up the West by providing reliable long-distance transport. They were also a lifeline for frontier towns.

And they took western produce to markets in eastern cities.

RAILROAD tunnels were blasted through mountain ranges. Workers used gunpowder, picks and shovels.

BUILDING tunnels was dangerous work. Hundreds of men died in blast accidents and rock falls.

TUNNEL building began by digging a central shaft.

GALLERIES were blasted each side.

A SMALL locomotive provided haulage power.

LUMPS of rock were hauled up to the surface.

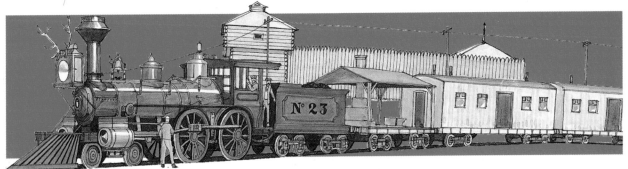

Facts about Railroads:

Railroads brought longed-for mail to pioneers' families and friends. Post office staff hoisted a flag to signal the arrival of new mail.

Some buffalo-hunters went shooting from special trains. As the train crossed the prairies, they lowered the windows and shot the buffalo.

More than 12,000 workers migrated from China to work on the Central Pacific railroad.

RAIL STATIONS were important to frontier towns, because railroads were one of their only links with the rest of the world. As well as mail and passengers, trains brought books and newspapers out to the West.

LOCOMOTIVES burned wood as fuel. They were fitted with wide 'bell' funnels to catch sparks and prevent prairie grass fires. In front there were cow-catchers and, in winter, snow plows, too. The first railroad journeys were uncomfortable and cold, but companies soon introduced carriages with heating and padded seats. The first with reclining seats were introduced in 1876.

THERE were great celebrations (below) when the east and west coasts of America were linked by railroad in 1869. The track was 1,772 miles long.

FACT: SHOPS HAD FALSE FRONTS SO THEY LOOKED BIGGER

IN THE 1850S this town was just a huddle of one-room huts, housing miners and pioneer families staking their claims to prairie land. There was a muddy main street, a general store and a few shabby bars. Now, 30 years later, it is thriving. It has better houses, several kinds of shop, a school, chapel, stockyard, corn store and a railroad station. Professional people have opened offices: a doctor, a dentist and a lawyer.

Facts about Frontier Towns:
Sheriffs kept order in frontier towns. Gunfights were rare.

Towns thrived as more people came to the West. But many poor farmers still had to barter (swap) home-made produce for goods.

Streets were filthy. Shopkeepers built boardwalks to keep customers' feet clean.

THE GENERAL STORE sold almost everything, from coffee and sugar to boots, Bibles, tin baths and paraffin lamps.

boardwalk

stagecoach

THE STAGECOACH passed through the town every 10 days, taking passengers and mail along the wild roads that linked the frontier towns and forts.

THE SALOON was a meeting place, as well as a bar. Next door stood a bank, which loaned money to farmers to buy tools and seeds. Many farmers spent all their lives in debt. Visitors to the town stayed at the hotel. Every Sunday there were services and Bible classes at the new church.

THE BLACKSMITH made and mended farm tools, and carried out emergency repairs to passing stage-coaches and wagons. But his main work was shoeing farm horses, oxen and mules.

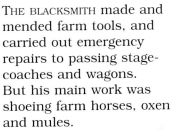

windmill to raise water

church

barber's shop

milliner's shop

FARMERS' wives made most of their clothes, but visiting the milliner's was a chance to gossip and admire the latest fashions.

FACT: THOUSANDS DIED IN THE WARS FOR THE WEST

URING THE 19TH-CENTURY 'Wars for the West', between about 1860 and 1890, farmers, ranchers, goldminers and US troops fought Native warriors, fenced their hunting grounds and plowed up the prairies. They also shot the buffalo and brought deadly diseases. As Chief Tatanka Yotanka (Sitting Bull) said: 'You have taken our land and made us outcasts.'

Even worse, the US government moved entire nations to 'Reservations'. There they could not hunt or farm, but had to struggle to survive on government rations. Children were sent away to European-style schools and forbidden to speak their own languages. Today we would call this 'genocide' – the deliberate murder of a people and their culture.

THE US GOVERNMENT sent officials to negotiate with Native leaders. They wanted Native peoples to agree to give up their land.

MANY nations were forced at gunpoint from their lands.

IN 1864, at Sand Creek, US soldiers killed 150 Native people, mostly women and children. Native American warriors could also be brutal, scalping and disemboweling their enemies.

By the 1870s European-Americans were killing over 3 million buffalo a year, almost exterminating the animal on which the Great Plains people depended.

US GENERAL George Custer (1839-1876) was criticized for his attacks on Native peoples.

CHIEF Tatanka Yotanka (1834-1890) lead the Dakota Sioux against Custer and his troops.

Facts on Wars for the West:

Native American Ghost Dancers who fought the Europeans wore magical painted shirts, which they believed would protect them from bullets. Sadly, they were wrong.

Over 50,000 Native Americans were killed in the Wars for the West.

The US government did not grant Native Americans full citizens' rights until 1924.

GHOST DANCERS hoped Native spirits would help them. But they were massacred at Wounded Knee in 1890.

GLOSSARY

Adze Tool with the blade at right angles to the handle, for shaping wood.

Cholera Disease causing sickness, diarrhea and death.

Linseed oil Oil made from the crushed seeds of the flax plant.

Nomads People who move their homes from place to place. Usually, they are hunters or cattle-herders.

Palisade Strong, defensive fence made of tree-trunks.

Pioneers In the American West, people who set out to make new lives for themselves in lands where Europeans and European-Americans had not settled before.

Prairie Open grassland.

Pueblo Village in south-western North America, made of several houses joined together.

Reservation Land set aside by the US government for Native Americans to live on when they had been expelled from their homelands.

Sod Slab of turf, shaped like a house-brick.

Sorghum Plant belonging to the grass and cane family. When boiled, the stems yield a sticky syrup.

Squash Plants of the marrow and pumpkin family.

Teepee Cone-shaped house made of buffalo skin arranged over wooden poles.

Tomahawk A small fighting axe.

Tornado A violent whirlwind, that destroys all trees and houses in its path.

Travois A wooden frame used to carry heavy loads, pulled by a horse or a dog.

Index